Getting to Know Allah Our Creator
A Children's Book Introducing Allah

by The Sincere Seeker **Kids** Collection

Allah is **One** & **Only**.
Allah is our **Creator**.
Allah controls and **Takes care** of You &
ME & our families & Everything else too.
Allah gives us food and a cozy warm
bed where we are safe & SOUND.
Allah is way UP Above the HEAVENS.

Allah created **big** planets and <small>small</small> **planets.**
Allah Created the Earth for us to live in.
Allah **created** shining bright stars to give us light.
Allah Created the Whole Universe.

Allah Created the FULL Moon.
Allah created the FLUFFY GREY CLOUDS.
Allah brings down rain to the Earth to feed it and clean it.
Allah makes the wind blow in different directions.
Allah makes the sun SHINE bright.

Allah Created cold water and hot water too.
Allah **created** beautiful blue Rivers.

Allah Created the BIG WAVY OCEANS.
Allah **created** the deep **dark** seas.

Allah makes the *waves* m o v e and r I s e.

Allah Created **tall** *Rocky*

Mountains.
Allah **created** **short** snowy Mountains.

Allah Created Banana trees &
Orange Trees for us to eat from.
Allah created beautiful smelling Flowers
of different kinds and colors for us to enjoy.

Allah Created Happy families to spend time together.
Allah Created loving Parents to take care of us and to love us & for us to be good to them.
Allah Created fun Brothers and Sisters to look after you and for you to look after them.

Allah Created **Big** Animals like the African Elephants And Brown Bears and Green Alligators with sharp *TEETH*.

Allah Created Small Animals like THE tiny ladybug and the buzzing bumble bee. Allah created jumpy grasshoppers, teeny-tiny ants, and flying dragonflies.

Allah Created nutritious food TO HELP OUR BODY GROW HEALTHY & STRONG.
ALLAH created tasty drinks for when you are thirsty.
Allah created purple grapes, yummy fresh bread, yellow cheese, juicy chicken, and delicious red apples.

Allah Gifts people Life & gifts them many things too.
Allah gifted us a comfortable home TO LIVE,
a car TO DRIVE, our favorite toys TO PLAY with,
both OUR hands to make things and both OUR feet to walk,
our eyes to see, our ears to hear, and our mouths to eat and talk.

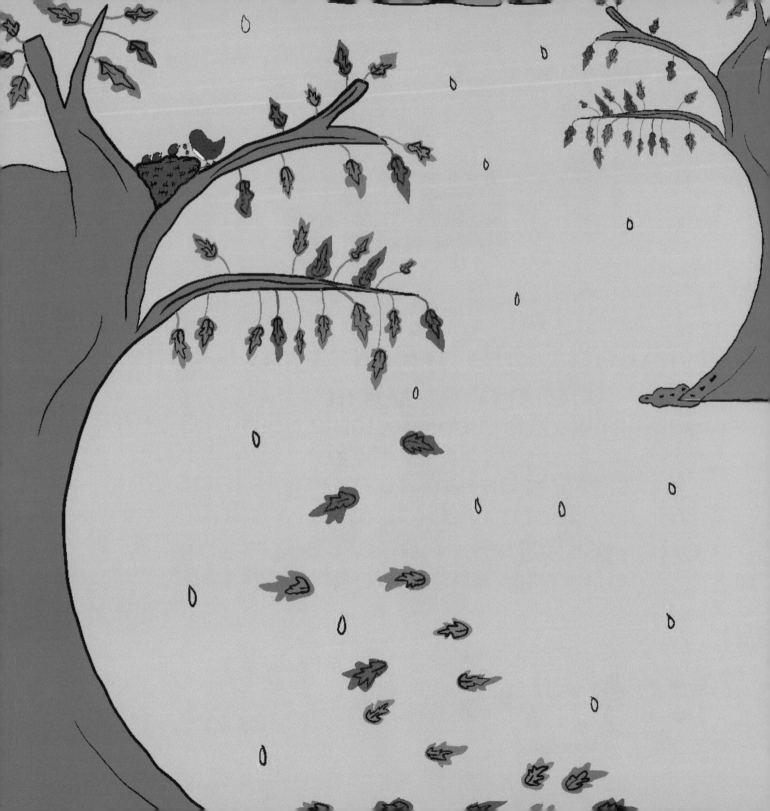

Allah Sees and knows everything that is happening. Allah **Hears everything that is being said.**

Allah is **Very** Loving.
Allah loves us **very, very** much.
Allah cares for us **very, very** much.
We should Love Him too.

All good is from Allah
Allah is the light of the heavens
and the earth.
Allah Puts Light in People's Hearts.

We Pray to Allah because ALLAH
Created us & Loves us.
and we love ALLAH too.
Allah Answers our dua prayers
when we ask Him.
We should always talk to Allah.

ALLAH will gift good people happy Paradise where they will get whatever they WISH for and live HAPPILY EVER AFTER.

The End.

Printed in Great Britain
by Amazon